PICTURE LIBRARY

AIRCRAFT CARRIERS

PICTURE LIBRARY
AIRCRAFT CARRIERS

C.J. Norman

Franklin Watts

London   New York   Sydney   Toronto

© 1986 Franklin Watts Ltd

First published in Great Britain
    1986 by
Franklin Watts Ltd
12a Golden Square
London W1R 4BA

First published in the USA by
Franklin Watts Inc
387 Park Avenue South
New York
N Y 10016

First published in Australia by
Franklin Watts
14 Mars Road
Lane Cove
2066 N.S.W.

UK ISBN: 0 86313 352 5
US ISBN: 0-531-10088-X
Library of Congress Catalog Card
Number: 85-51452

Printed in Italy
by Tipolitografia G. Canale & C. S.p.A. - Turin

Designed by
Barrett & Willard

Photographs by
British Aerospace
Fleet Photographic, Royal Navy
NATO
Naval Photographic Center, Washington DC
US Navy/MARS, Lincs

Illustration by
Janos Marffy/Jillian Burgess Artists

Technical Consultant
Bernard Fitzsimons

Series Editor
N.S. Barrett

Contents

Introduction

Aircraft carriers are the largest warships afloat. They have wide, flat decks from which warplanes take off. Jet bombers and fighters operate from these great floating airfields.

There are several classes of aircraft carrier. The largest can carry as many as 100 planes. Smaller aircraft carriers carry helicopters and jump-jets, which can take off from and land on a small deck.

△ USS *Nimitz*, an attack aircraft carrier of the US Navy, is one of the largest warships afloat.

Aircraft carriers are built for different purposes. The large US carriers such as the *Nimitz* are called attack carriers. An attack carrier operates in a fleet as part of an attack or defense group.

The latest British carriers were designed for hunting submarines. They operate with other anti-sub warships.

Some navies use assault ships which carry landing craft and helicopters for beach landings.

△ HMS *Invincible*, a multi-purpose British carrier, has been used for air defense and land assault work as well as anti-submarine duties.

The aircraft carrier

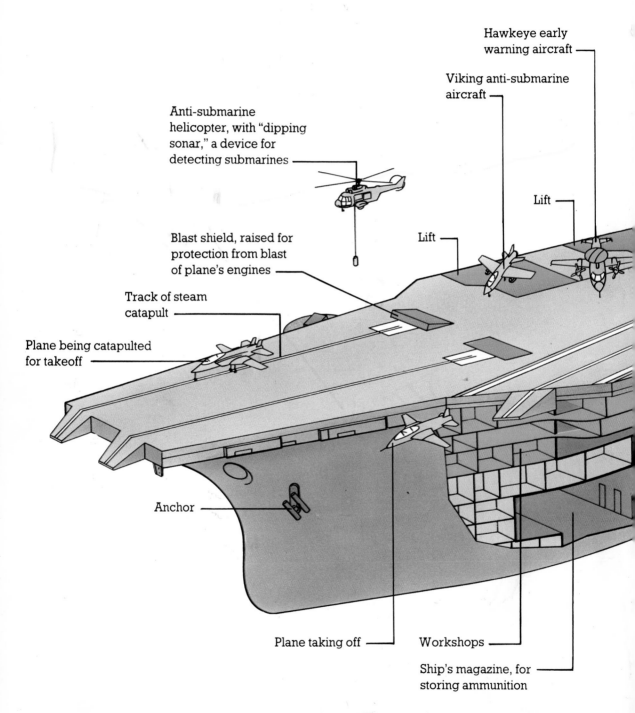

Hawkeye early
warning aircraft

Viking anti-submarine
aircraft

Anti-submarine
helicopter, with "dipping
sonar," a device for
detecting submarines

Lift

Blast shield, raised for
protection from blast
of plane's engines

Lift

Track of steam
catapult

Plane being catapulted
for takeoff

Anchor

Plane taking off

Workshops

Ship's magazine, for
storing ammunition

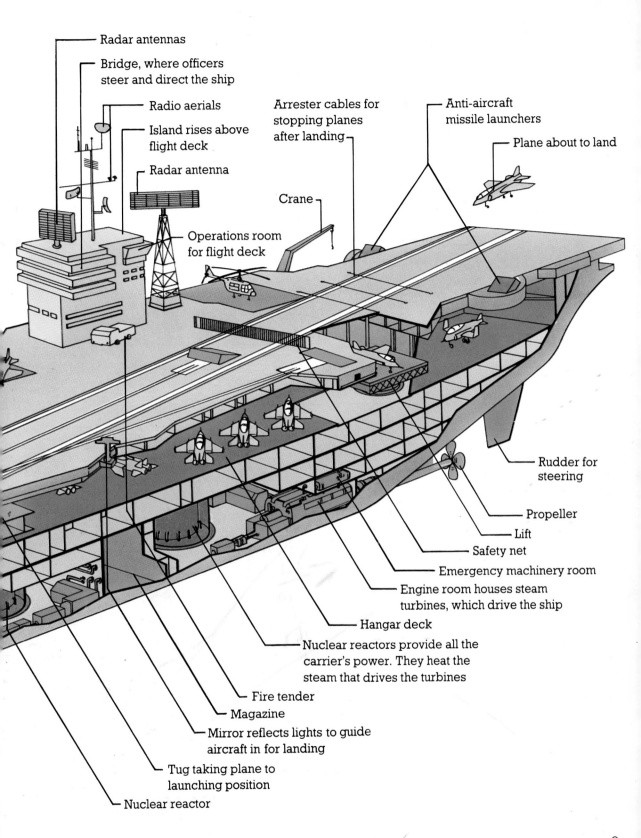

Radar antennas

Bridge, where officers steer and direct the ship

Radio aerials

Island rises above flight deck

Radar antenna

Arrester cables for stopping planes after landing

Anti-aircraft missile launchers

Plane about to land

Crane

Operations room for flight deck

Rudder for steering

Propeller

Lift

Safety net

Emergency machinery room

Engine room houses steam turbines, which drive the ship

Hangar deck

Nuclear reactors provide all the carrier's power. They heat the steam that drives the turbines

Fire tender

Magazine

Mirror reflects lights to guide aircraft in for landing

Tug taking plane to launching position

Nuclear reactor

Types of aircraft carriers

An attack carrier operates at the heart of a fleet. It is protected by the other ships in the fleet, and its planes provide protection for the fleet from enemy aircraft, submarines and other ships over a wide area.

The latest attack carriers are powered by nuclear fuel. They can operate for several years without refueling.

▽ USS *Midway* was built at the end of World War II, in 1945. It is the oldest attack carrier still in service in the US Navy. It has been refitted twice to bring it into line with modern carriers. It can carry more than 70 aircraft and 4,500 crew.

Modern attack carriers such as those of the Nimitz class cost over 4 billion dollars to build. This does not include the cost of the 90 to 100 aircraft carried.

They have a crew of more than 6,000. Of these, over 2,500 are concerned with the operation and maintenance of the aircraft.

▽ **USS** *Forrestal* steams into port. The Forrestal class ships were the first US carriers built after World War II. There are four ships in this class, the others being the *Saratoga*, *Ranger*, and *Independence*. They carry up to 85 aircraft and have a crew of about 5,400.

◁ USS *Dwight D. Eisenhower* is the second ship in the Nimitz class. It came into service in 1977. Carriers of this class are the largest warships in the world. They are powered by nuclear fuel, which gives them the ability to sail for almost a million nautical miles without the need to refuel.

Nimitz class carriers carry up to 100 aircraft, but not all of them can be kept in the hangars below deck. The ships carry enough fuel and aviation stores for the aircraft to be operated for up to 16 days continuously.

These great warships have three sets of missile launchers, but no guns. They are protected by other warships of the fleet and by their own aircraft.

The rods that can be seen sticking out at the sides of the ship are radio aerials.

Anti-submarine aircraft carriers use helicopters to search for submarines and destroy them. The helicopters use sonar, a sound echo system, to detect submarines.

Jump-jet fighters are carried for air defense. They patrol a wide area around the carrier, ready to fight off enemy reconnaissance or strike aircraft.

Two views of Invincible class carriers of the British Royal Navy. The sloping deck at the bow, or front, of each ship is to assist aircraft to take off. Helicopters are used for hunting submarines, and Sea Harriers provide air defense. The ships carry about 14 of these jump-jets.
△ HMS *Ark Royal*.
▷ HMS *Illustrious*.

Assault carriers transport troops to landing points. They have about 20 to 30 helicopters for landing troops. Landing craft put vehicles as well as troops on shore.

Jump-jets may be used to support the landing by attacking the defenses on shore. The carriers have anti-aircraft weapons, but their main defense is provided by other ships.

△ USS *Iwo Jima*, the first of its class. This class was the first designed especially to operate helicopters. There are seven ships in the class. Each one can carry about 30 helicopters and 2,000 assault troops, and has a crew of more than 600. Iwo Jima class vessels are also known as "amphibious assault ships."

Injured troops may be picked up by helicopter and ferried back to the carrier. Assault carriers have hospitals equipped with operating rooms and as many as 300 beds. They also have workshops for repairing vehicles and equipment.

Helicopter gunships operate from assault carriers when needed to support the landing. They provide cover for their troops and attack enemy tanks and strong-points.

▽ USS *Tarawa*, the first of a class of general purpose amphibious assault ships. There are five carriers in the class. These large amphibious assault ships can land 1,900 troops, 5 battle tanks, 6 big field guns, and 11 large amphibious assault vehicles, as well as carry more than 20 helicopters. Note the carrier's straight sides, allowing more space for cargo.

Takeoff and landing

Aircraft take off from carriers by means of a device called a steam catapult. The planes are attached by hooks to runners that slide along tracks on the deck. Steam is used to shoot the runners forward at great speed and then the plane is launched into the air.

Some catapults work by a strong spring or an explosive charge.

▽ Launched by a catapult, a Tomcat takes off from the deck of an aircraft carrier.

For landing, an aircraft lowers a hook under its tail point which catches on one of the "arrester" cables stretched across the deck. The cable moves along with the plane and is slowed down by a braking system.

On some carriers, planes can be stopped in as little as 100 yards (90 m). There is a safety net beyond the cables for emergencies.

▽ A Hornet aircraft (top) comes in to land on USS *Enterprise*. It is about to hook on to one of the cables that can be seen stretched out in front of it across the deck. A Phantom jet (below) makes a barrier landing. A netting-type barrier is positioned behind the cables in case all of them are missed.

▷ Two Hornets are prepared for takeoff from USS *Constellation*.

The catapult tracks can be clearly seen in front of the planes. The tracks are at a slight angle to each other, so that the aircraft do not take off in exactly the same direction.

The barrier behind the plane on the left is a blast shield. This is raised just before the plane is about to take off to protect crew or other aircraft from the blast of the engines.

Some smaller carriers, such as those of the Invincible class, use a raised ramp to assist takeoff (see top picture). This allows the aircraft to carry heavier loads.

Helicopters and some special aircraft need very little space for taking off and landing. Helicopters take off and land straight up and down.

Special planes take off with little or no forward speed. They also land vertically, or straight downward. A plane with this capability is called a VTOL aircraft. This stands for Vertical TakeOff and Landing.

△ A helicopter comes in to land on the deck of an aircraft carrier.

▷ A jump-jet aircraft (left) prepares to land on USS *Guam*, an assault carrier of the Iwo Jima class. The platforms on each side of the deck are lifts, which raise aircraft from the hangar deck to the flight deck.

Above and below deck

The island of a carrier is on its starboard side, the right-hand side looking forward. The rest of the flight deck is left clear for planes.

Below the flight deck is the hangar deck, where the aircraft are stored and maintained.

Other decks house the crew's living quarters as well as storage space for ammunition and supplies.

△ A crewman checks the ship's position on an instrument called a sextant.

▷ There is plenty of room (top) for off-duty crewmen to sunbathe on the deck of a large attack carrier.

A radio operator (bottom) tunes in a receiver.

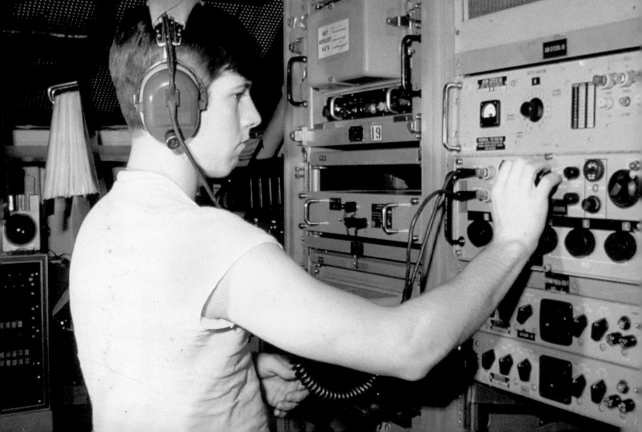

◁ A Tomcat aircraft stands on the lift ready to be raised onto the flight deck of the nuclear-powered carrier USS *Dwight D. Eisenhower.*

The plane's wings are folded. Aircraft are stored on the hangar deck with folded wings to save space.

The bright red and yellow stripes round the top of the lift act as a warning to crew on the flight deck.

The story of carriers

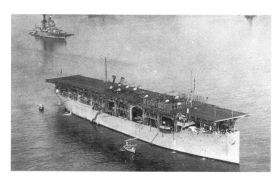

△ USS *Langley*, converted from a coal ship in the 1920s.

The first aircraft carriers

HMS *Argus*, which was originally designed as a liner, was completed as a carrier in 1918. It could carry 20 planes. The first US carrier was the *Langley*, converted from a collier, or coal ship, in 1922.

Two more US carriers, the *Lexington* and the *Saratoga*, were built on battle-cruiser hulls. They joined the fleet in 1927, and were then the biggest and fastest carriers afloat.

The first ship to be designed as an aircraft carrier was HMS *Hermes*, completed in 1923. It was sunk by Japanese aircraft in World War II.

Carriers at war

Aircraft carriers were the most important ships of World War II (1939–45). The warring nations built more than 150 carriers.

The Battle of Midway, in 1942, proved to be a turning point in the war. Midway, in the pacific Ocean, consists of two islands, held by the United States since 1867. US land- and carrier-based planes engaged the Japanese fleet off Midway in June of 1942. In winning their first decisive naval victory of the war with Japan, they sank four Japanese carriers.

In all, during the war, over 40 carriers were sunk, nearly half of them by submarines.

△ HMS *Ark Royal*, a famous British carrier of the early years of World War II, was sunk in 1941. It was bigger and faster than the modern carrier named after it.

Bigger and better

After the war, the United States built more aircraft carriers. These were bigger and better than the ones that had served them so well during the war, most of which were scrapped.

△ USS *Carl Vinson*, a Nimitz class carrier that came into service in 1982.

Only the Midway class of the war-built carriers are still in service.

With more than a dozen attack carriers in service, the US Navy has far more than any other navy. The four carriers of the Forrestal class were built in the 1950s. USS *Enterprise*, the only ship of its class, came into service in 1961 and was the first nuclear-powered aircraft carrier.

The four ships of the Kitty Hawk class, developed from the Forrestal class, came into service in the 1960s. The latest US carriers are nuclear-powered vessels of the Nimitz class. The first of these, USS *Nimitz*, came into service in 1975.

The only ships that approach the size of the large US carriers are those of the Soviet Kiev class, the first of which was commissioned in the mid-1970s, and the French Clemenceau class (1960s).

Light carriers

Smaller, lighter carriers have been built for assault and anti-submarine duties. Most of these are US carriers, including the Tarawa class of assault ships and the Iwo Jima carrier class, the first to be built specially to operate helicopters.

Some British carriers were adapted for different purposes. The *Hermes*, for example, started life in the late 1950s as an attack carrier, and in the 1970s was converted first to an assault carrier and then to an anti-submarine carrier.

Three smaller, multi-purpose carriers of the Invincible class have also come into service with the British Royal Navy in the 1980s.

△ A Sea Harrier jump-jet comes in to land on HMS *Hermes*, one of the carriers that saw service for Britain in the Falklands War.

Facts and records

Largest warship

The three Nimitz class aircraft carriers – the *Nimitz*, *Dwight D Eisenhower*, and *Vinson* – are the largest warships afloat, measured in displacement tonnage. This is the amount of water displaced, or occupied, by a ship. The Nimitz class carriers displace nearly 105,000 tons.

△ USS *Enterprise*, the world's longest aircraft carrier.

Longest carrier

The Nimitz class carriers are 1,092 ft (332.8 m) long, but they are not quite the longest warships afloat. This distinction belongs to USS *Enterprise*, which measures 1,123 ft (342.3 m) from stem to stern.

First flight from a ship

In November 1910 Eugene Ely, a US aviation pioneer, took off in his Curtiss biplane from a platform built USS *Birmingham* light cruiser. This was the first ever flight on record to take off from a ship.

Two months later Ely made the first landing on a ship when he set his plane down on a platform built on the *Pennsylvania*, a cruiser.

Seaplane carriers

In 1914, after the outbreak of World War I, some British passenger steamers were equipped to carry seaplanes. The flimsy aircraft were protected by canvas hangars and lifted in and out of the water by crane.

Late starters

The Soviet Union completed its first aircraft carrier in 1975. The *Kiev* was the first of a class about the same size as the US Tarawa carriers.

△ Soviet aircraft carriers, such as the *Kiev*, are heavily armed.

Glossary

Amphibious assault ship
A carrier used for landing troops and fighting vehicles on shore.

Arrester cables
Large, metal cables stretched across the deck of a carrier to assist aircraft landing. The plane lowers a hook, which catches on one of the cables.

Blast shield
A flap on the deck of a carrier, behind the steam catapult. It is raised when a plane is ready to take off. It deflects the blast from the plane's engines.

Hangar deck
The deck below the flight deck. Aircraft are stored there.

Helicopter gunship
A heavily armed helicopter, used for attack with guns or missiles.

Jump-jet
Another term for a VTOL jet.

Lift
Lifts are used to move aircraft from one deck level to another.

Nautical mile
The unit used for measuring distances at sea. A nautical mile is equivalent to 1.15 statute (land) miles or 1.85 km.

Reconnaissance aircraft
Planes whose task is to locate and report back on enemy positions.

Sextant
An instrument used for finding the position of a ship at sea. It measures the angle between the sun or a star and the horizon.

Starboard
The right-hand side of a ship looking forward.

Steam catapult
A device used to launch aircraft from the deck of a carrier.

Stern
The back of a ship.

Strike aircraft
Planes that attack other ships or land targets.

VTOL
An aircraft that can take off vertically (straight up) or with very little forward motion, and can land vertically. The letters stand for Vertical TakeOff and Landing.

Index